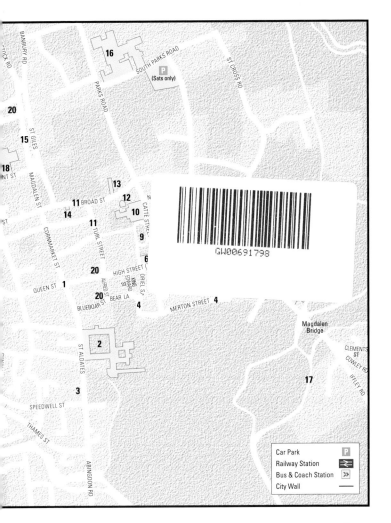

Map Ref

All information correct at time of going to press but may be subject to change. Some colleges are free to visit and some charge an admission fee. Maximum numbers in visiting parties may apply. Normal opening hours may be affected by special university events, exams etc. To avoid disappointment, check with the relevant college or institution in advance of your visit.

▶ Carfax and Cornmarket

A crossroads stands at Oxford's ancient heart, leading north, south, east and west. Its name – Carfax – probably derives from the Latin *quadrifurcus* meaning 'four forks'. The crossroads is marked by Carfax Tower or, more correctly, St Martin's Tower as this is all that remains of a church that jutted into Cornmarket Street from 1032. The 'Roman' quarterboys on the tower's clock are replicas of the 17th-century originals that can be seen in the Museum of Oxford.

A recurring problem over the years has been how to ease the flow of traffic through this small and busy crossroads and each century seems to have brought its own problems. An open-air market had congested the crossroads since medieval times and was moved in the late 18th century. Around this time a large, stone conduit (supplying water, or wine on special occasions) was also removed. It had stood at the centre of Carfax since 1617. St Martin's Church was rebuilt when the medieval structures proved unsafe but was demolished in 1896. Despite these earlier attempts to clear the thoroughfare, the traffic and pollution levels of the 20th century resulted in a restructured traffic flow in 1999. Cornmarket Street, usually referred to as just 'Cornmarket', is Oxford's main shopping street and is now reclaimed for pedestrians.

Oxford's oldest building, the Saxon tower of St Michael at the North Gate, stands on the corner of Cornmarket and Ship Street. The Oxford Martyrs – Thomas Cranmer, Hugh Latimer and Nicholas Ridley – were incarcerated in the former Bocardo prison here, and the door of their cell can be seen in the tower. Over 300 years later, in 1859, William and Jane Morris were married in St Michael's. Both Carfax Tower and the tower of St Michael at the North Gate offer superb views over the city.

Carfax Tower
Open: Easter–Oct: Daily 1000–
        1700
St Michael's Tower
Tel: 01865 240940
Open: Apr–Oct: Mon–Sat 1000–
        1700, Sun 1200–1700;
        Nov–Mar: Mon–Sat 1000–
        1600, Sun 1200–1600

Christ Church and the Cathedral

Frideswide was an 8th-century princess and nun who founded a priory on the site of which Oxford's cathedral now stands. The priory was burned to the ground in 1002 and an Augustinian priory replaced it in 1122. Cardinal Thomas Wolsey dissolved the priory, intending to transform it into 'Cardinal College'. On Wolsey's fall from power, Henry VIII took over the project. The priory chapel became a cathedral, which was combined with the college, receiving the name Christ Church in 1546. The cloisters date from the 15th century, but the west side was destroyed to make way for the largest of all the city's quadrangles. Tom Quad is a testament to Wolsey's vision for the college. He completed three-quarters of it; the fourth side and the mighty Tom Tower were added in the 17th century. The tower houses Great Tom, the bell that rings out 101 times (signifying the original number of students) at 9.05 every night (the time by which they should be back in college) and is named not after Wolsey, but Thomas à Becket. Henry VIII had ordered the destruction of all monuments to Becket, but the martyr is depicted in the 14th-century glass in St Lucy's Chapel. Much of the later stained glass in the cathedral is the work of William Morris and Edward Burne-Jones.

Pass through classical Peckwater Quad to Canterbury Quad which contains the entrance to the Picture Gallery. The gallery contains old masters including works by Tintoretto and Van Dyck, and a Holbein portrait of Henry VIII.

Only the protests of both academics and townspeople saved Christ Church Meadow from the 'relief road' mooted by the council and approved by the government of the day. Fortunately it was saved, so cattle may continue to graze and people may continue to stroll in this most tranquil of spaces.

Tel: 01865 276150
Open: Out of term: normally 0900–1700; In term: Mon–Sat 0900–1730, Sun 1245–1730, cathedral 0900–1645, hall will close at 1145 and reopen at 1430 (only open from 1430 on Sat); to confirm opening times check with the head custodian (tel: 01865 276492)

Alice Liddell was the daughter of the Dean of Christ Church and Charles Dodgson was a tutor at the college. Under the pen-name Lewis Carroll, Dodgson wrote *Alice's Adventures in Wonderland* and *Through the Looking-Glass*. Lovers of these classic children's stories will find that Alice's Oxford and her Wonderland were closer than they might expect.

References to people or places that Alice knew are scattered throughout Lewis Carroll's tales. John Ruskin was Alice's drawing master and appears as an 'old conger eel', her governess Miss Prickett becomes the bossy Red Queen and Dodgson associated himself with the Dodo. Alice's sisters Lorina and Edith became the Lory and the Eaglet. It is Edith's face that Burne-Jones depicted in the St Catherine window in the cathedral's Regimental Chapel.

Christ Church is known to its members as 'The House' (from *Aedes Christi* – the House of Christ) and Alice threatens to set her cat at the White Rabbit when he suggests burning 'the house down'. The 'treacle well' in the Dormouse's story refers to a real well at St Margaret's Church, Binsey. 'Treacle' in medieval times indicated a healing liquid and St Margaret's was both the scene of a miracle performed by Frideswide and a place of pilgrimage in the Middle Ages. The well is depicted in Burne-Jones' St Frideswide window in the cathedral.

In *Through the Looking-Glass* Alice meets a fawn in the wood 'where things have no names' and walks with her arms 'clasped lovingly' round its neck. When the fawn remembers Alice is human it starts away, just as the real deer would have done on one of Alice's visits to Magdalen Deer Park.

The shop in St Aldate's where Alice used to buy barley sugar was transformed into the Old Sheep Shop in *Through the Looking-Glass*. It is now called Alice's Shop and is a veritable treasure trove of delightful Alice memorabilia. Alice's Gallery and Tearoom, a relative newcomer to the city, is housed in premises just a few doors down.

ALICE'S SHOP

Alice's Shop	
Tel:	01865 723793
Open:	Daily 1100–1700
Alice's Gallery and Tearoom	
Open:	Tue–Sun 1100–1700

Merton Street and Oriel Square

There are pockets of Oxford where time appears to have wrought few changes. The atmosphere of the medieval university is most strongly evoked in cobbled Merton Street. Merton College (founded in 1264) is one of three that claim to be the oldest in Oxford; the others are Balliol (which may have had an early community of scholars but was not formally endowed until later) and University (on the doubtful grounds that it was founded by Alfred the Great). Walter de Merton, the college's founder, was chancellor of England under Henry III and it is the figures of these two men that adorn the gate-tower. At their feet is a 15th-century woodland scene depicting St John the Baptist, birds and beasts, and the kneeling figure of Walter de Merton. The exquisite medieval library is reached via Oxford's oldest quad, 14th-century Mob Quad.

The Front Quad at Corpus Christi College is dominated by the unusual sundial, which dates from 1581. The pelican on top of the sundial is both the college emblem and a symbol of Christ's sacrifice, pecking at her own breast to feed her young. A perpetual calendar, dating from 1606, is on the pillar below.

Oriel Square with its 18th-century houses is reputedly one of the most filmed places in Oxford. An oriel window is a projecting upper-floor window and one of Oriel College's original buildings, La Oriole, had this feature. The Jacobean-Gothic front quad testifies to the strength of university support for Charles II during the English Civil War; the words over the staircase read *Regnante Carolo* – 'When Charles reigns'. Unfortunately, Oriel College is closed to the public.

Merton College
Tel: 01865 276310
Open: Mon–Fri 1400–1600,
          Sat–Sun 1000–1600; tours
          of the library in summer
          months Mon–Sat only
          (check before visiting)
Corpus Christi College
Tel: 01865 276700
Open: Daily 1330–1630

William Wordsworth called it 'glorious' and Nikolaus Pevsner thought it 'one of the world's great streets'. Oxford's High Street – or 'The High' – is a blend of architectural styles gracing a sublime curve.

Leaving Carfax, the beautiful 17th-century timber-framed Kemp Hall is on the right, now housing the Thai restaurant, Chiang Mai Kitchen. On the left is the Covered Market, which has been on the site since 1774, although it was rebuilt and roofed over in the 1890s. The market is a vibrant mix of butchers', florists', delicatessens and boutiques.

Further down, you will find University College on the right and The Queen's College on the left. University College contains two very similar Jacobean-Gothic quads – Front Quad and Radcliffe Quad. A poignant memorial to Percy Bysshe Shelley can be reached via the northwest corner of the Front Quad.

The Queen's College is an example of Oxford tradition at work; note that the correct term is 'The' Queen's, rather than just 'Queen's'. Similarly, Christ Church is never called Christ Church College and although it is fine to refer to Magdalen (pronounced 'maudlin'), Merton or Wadham, you should never call New College simply 'New'. The queen in question is Queen Philippa of Hainault, consort to Edward III, but the statue under the cupola at the gate is Queen Caroline who supplied funds for the 18th-century rebuilding.

In June, the High Street is peppered with students in black and white 'subfusc', the formal outfit that they must wear to sit their exams. The neo-Jacobean Examination Schools have a frontage onto the High, but it is worth turning down Merton Street to see the finest aspect of the building.

Oxford's Botanic Garden, opposite Magdalen College, is the oldest physic garden in Britain and the third oldest in the world.

The Queen's College
Tel: 01865 279121
Access: 1400–1630 only with an
         official Blue Badge Guide
         booked at the Tourist
         Information Centre
         (tel: 01865 726871)
University College
Closed except by special arrangement with the domestic bursar
(tel: 01865 276625)

▶ University Church of St Mary the Virgin

The church of St Mary the Virgin has been associated with the university since its earliest history, when it was used for meetings, disputations and degree ceremonies. It was here that Thomas Cranmer received the final verdict before he was burned at the stake and here that John Keble preached a sermon that led to the birth of the Oxford Movement. The charismatic leader of the Movement, John Henry Newman, was vicar of St Mary's and became something of a cult figure among his followers who affected his speech and dress.

During the frequent struggles between 'town and gown', the scholars would rally their forces by ringing the bells of St Mary's while the bells of St Martin at Carfax summoned the townspeople. Whatever the outcome of these clashes, the upshot would invariably be the same – that the university (usually backed by the monarchy and the Church) would be victorious.

The south porch is an ornate example of English Baroque, but the church's most interesting features are its 13th-century tower and 14th-century spire. Of the four viewpoints in Oxford, this has the most difficult climb, but you are rewarded with outstanding views across the heart of the university (above). In 1320, the Congregation House was built to provide a place for the university's governing body to meet. Today the Convocation Coffee House is situated in the lower room of the old Congregation House.

Tel: 01865 279111
Open: Sun 1215–1700
Sep–Jun: Mon–Sat 0900–1700; Jul–Aug: Mon–Sat 0900–1900 (Coffee House opens 1000 and Jul–Aug closes 1800)

Tel: 01865 276000
Open: Daily 1400–dusk

► Magdalen College

One of Oxford's oldest jokes is that visitors often arrive and ask to see the 'university'. Of course, with no central campus and dozens of colleges dotted around the city, this is not a simple request. Many of the colleges are worthy of a visit; each has its own charms and features. However, if you have only a short time in Oxford, you should not miss Christ Church, New College and Magdalen College.

Magdalen College was founded in 1458 and is home to some of Oxford's finest architecture. It is from the beautiful bell tower that the choir sing an invocation to summer at 6 o' clock on May Morning. The tradition probably dates back to the tower's inauguration in 1509 and today is accompanied by celebration in the streets with morris men and street performers. The heart of the college is the 15th-century Cloister Quadrangle which leads to the neoclassical New Buildings. Behind these is Magdalen Grove Deer Park, home to the college's herd of fallow deer. A stroll along Addison's Walk will take you around a meadow that in April is full of rare snakeshead fritillaries. The walk was named after Joseph Addison, the poet and essayist, whose rooms at the college overlooked the meadows.

Other great alumni include Oscar Wilde, who learned of his First while having breakfast at the Mitre and remembered Oxford as 'the most flower-like time of one's life', and C.S. Lewis, who was a Fellow of the college for 36 years. One of Lewis' students was John Betjeman, who – knowing that there was no-one to teach it – cheekily chose to study medieval Welsh, resulting in a tutor coming from Wales once a week just for him. Betjeman also aspired to Aestheticism but did not achieve Wilde's success, leaving without a degree.

Queen's Lane and New College Lane

The winding lane that links the High Street with the northern side of the city is a haven of quiet and full of the spirit of ancient Oxford.

Turning past the Queen's Lane Coffee House (one of Oxford's oldest coffee houses) into Queen's Lane, you approach St Edmund Hall on the right. 'Teddy Hall' is the only one of the former medieval academic halls to survive as a college and has a small and attractive Front Quad. Visitors can ask at the lodge for permission to see the stained glass by Morris and Burne-Jones in the chapel and for access to the intriguing crypt of St Peter in the East, now the college library.

Queen's Lane twists and turns into New College Lane, which is said to be haunted. Is the ghostly sound of horses' hooves an echo of the English Civil War, when Royalist forces assembled here before battle?

New College, founded in 1379, is one of Oxford's treasures. Its fabric incorporates part of the 13th-century city wall, an exquisite college chapel, evocative cloisters (pictured below) and gardens that Nathaniel Hawthorne referred to as 'indescribably beautiful'. New College's best-known alumnus was the Revd William Spooner who had a habit of transposing the first letters of certain words. Phrases such as 'Which of us has not felt in his heart a half-warmed fish?' have given us the term 'spoonerism', although Spooner admitted that he often used the technique to make others laugh and many spoonerisms are falsely attributed to him.

St Edmund Hall
Tel: 01865 279000
Open: Daily 0900–dusk
New College
Tel: 01865 279555
Open: Easter–Oct: Daily
         1100–1700 (entrance via
         gate-tower); Winter: Daily
         1400–1600 (entrance via
         Holywell Street)
Hertford College
Tel: 01865 279400
Open: Daily 1000–1200,
         1400–dusk (closed over
         the Christmas period)

New College Lane continues past the house of celebrated astronomer Edmund Halley to pass under the Bridge of Sighs. This graceful structure was designed by T.G. Jackson and links the north and south sides of Hertford College. Evelyn Waugh was at Hertford College and painted a traditional picture of privileged undergraduate life in *Brideshead Revisited*.

Radcliffe Square

James Gibbs was the architect responsible for the majestic Radcliffe Camera, although Nicholas Hawksmoor had proposed its circular form. The Camera (meaning 'chamber') was built to house an independent library devoted to the sciences and was the first round library in the world. Now a private reading room for the Bodleian, the Camera is only open to the public as part of a special extended tour (see information panel on p.13).

Two colleges flank the east and west sides of Radcliffe Square: All Souls and Brasenose. All Souls is unique in that it is only open to Fellows, and Fellowships are only awarded to those of the very highest academic ability. Its strikingly beautiful North Quadrangle features twin towers designed by Hawksmoor and a magnificent sundial by Christopher Wren.

Brasenose College was built on the site of a number of academic halls, one of which was known as Brasenose Hall. The hall gate had a brass knocker in the shape of an animal's face (the 'brazen nose'). In the 1330s the knocker was stolen by a group of tutors and students who tried to set up a rival university in Lincolnshire. The escapees returned to Oxford, leaving the knocker behind. The Oxford college had to wait until 1890 before the Lincolnshire building came up for sale and the whole could be purchased – thus recapturing the knocker that had been missing for over 500 years. The original is now situated in the hall and a replica hangs above the college gate.

All Souls College
Tel: 01865 279379
Open: Mon–Fri 1400–1600
         (parties of more than six
         need permission from the
         bursar)
Brasenose College
Tel: 01865 277830
Open: Daily 1000–1130 and
         1400–1630

Bodleian Library and Divinity School

A detailed Oxford map will indicate the Bodleian Library as a group of buildings around a quadrangle. A tour will reveal the exquisite Duke Humfrey's Library above the Divinity School. But this comes nowhere near explaining the magnitude of Thomas Bodley's life-work, for his Library is all around you – in the New Bodleian on the corner of Parks Road, in smaller libraries around the city and on miles of shelving under Broad Street and Radcliffe Square. It is said that the reason you cannot walk on the grass in Radcliffe Square is because it is only nine inches down to the roof of the book-stacks below.

Duke Humfrey's Library is the oldest part, having been finished in c.1489. However, it was neglected and ransacked and in 1598 Bodley resolved to devote his life and capital to its revival. The Bodleian is a copyright library – therefore it receives a copy of every book published – and no book can ever be taken away. Charles I and Cromwell were both refused permission and the explorer Richard Burton dedicated his translation of *Thousand and One Nights* to the library's curators when they forbade him to borrow a manuscript.

The Old Schools Quadrangle was started in 1613 when the collection needed more room and was designed to provide lecture rooms below and library space above. The names of the original schools (faculties) are painted above the doorways. The gate-tower is known as the Tower of the Five Orders because the decorative columns are, in rising tiers, embellished with the five orders of classical styles.

Tel: 01865 277224
Guided tours of the Divinity School, Convocation House and Duke Humfrey's Library: Nov–Mar: Mon–Fri at 1400, 1500; Sat 1030, 1130; Apr–Oct: as Nov–Mar plus Mon–Fri 1030, 1130. Special extended tours to incorporate the Upper Reading Room, Radcliffe Camera, underground mechanical book conveyor and New Bodleian book-stack can be booked up to 10 days in advance of your visit.

The construction of the Divinity School took about 60 years, funded by public subscription. The magnificent lierne-vaulted ceiling (below) is similar to that in the cathedral's 15th-century choir.

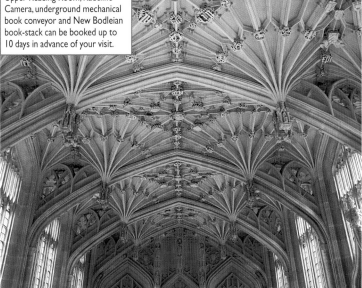

Broad Street and Turl Street

Balliol is one of the Oxford colleges that claim to be the city's oldest, asserting that John Balliol founded it in 1263 – however, the statutes were not drawn up until 1282. The medieval buildings were destroyed in a 19th-century rebuilding programme and the rather uninspiring result is generally considered to be in marked contrast to the luminaries the college has produced. Alumni include politicians such as Harold Macmillan and Roy Jenkins, the poet Gerard Manley Hopkins and writer Graham Greene.

Trinity College is next door to Balliol, with a delicate ironwork gate revealing inviting expanses of lawn. The college occupies the site of the former Durham College, founded in 1286 so that the monks of Durham Abbey had a place to live while studying in Oxford. The Baroque chapel contains a beautifully carved reredos.

Exeter is the first college on the left as you turn into Turl Street. The chapel was designed by George Gilbert Scott and is influenced by the Sainte Chapelle in Paris. There is a wealth of stained glass in the chapel, and the tapestry depicting the Adoration of the Magi was designed by Burne-Jones and made by Morris' firm (both artists were at Exeter College). Fans of Inspector Morse may know that it is in the quad outside the chapel that Morse finally collapses in *The Remorseful Day*.

Opposite Exeter is Jesus College, known in the past as the Welsh college because its founder was one Hugh Price of Brecon and until the late 19th century it took many students from Welsh grammar schools. One of the exceptions was T.E. Lawrence ('Lawrence of Arabia'), a bust of whom stands in the college chapel.

The view down Turl Street is enhanced at the south end by the spire of All Saints Church, now Lincoln College library. While some college architecture has suffered as a result of rebuilding programmes, Lincoln's relative poverty means that it has preserved an unspoiled charm.

Balliol College
Tel: 01865 277777
Open: Daily 1400–1700

Trinity College
Tel: 01865 279900
Open: Daily 1030–1200 and
       1400–1600 (weekends
       only in winter months)

Exeter College
Tel: 01865 279600
Open: Summer: Daily 1400–1700;
       Winter: Daily 1400–dusk

Jesus College
Tel: 01865 279700
Open: Daily 1400–1630

Lincoln College
Tel: 01865 279800
Open: Mon–Sat 1400–1700,
       Sun 1100–1700

Sheldonian Theatre
Tel: 01865 277299
Open: Mon–Sat 1000–1230 and
        1400–1630 (opening hours
        will be curtailed when the
        theatre is in use for univer-
        sity ceremonies, meetings
        or concerts)
Museum of the History of Science
Tel: 01865 277280
Open: Tue–Sat 1200–1600

Sheldonian Theatre

When Christopher Wren was commissioned to design the Sheldonian Theatre, he was Professor of Astronomy, but not recognized as an architect. It was felt that St Mary's was no longer a suitable place to hold university ceremonies – the unruliness of these occasions was deemed inappropriate in a religious building. Wren created a new arena – a vast classical space where the view of proceedings was not interrupted by roof-supporting pillars. In 1669 Robert Streeter was commissioned to paint the magnificent ceiling. It depicts a cloth being pulled back to reveal an open sky, illustrating the *Triumph of Religion, Arts and Science over Envy, Hate and Malice*. Climb to the rooftop cupola to be rewarded with one of Oxford's four aerial viewpoints.

As well as providing a setting for university events, including the colourful 'Encaenia' ceremony in June, the Sheldonian is used for concerts. Other venues for music lovers in the city include the Holywell Music Room (the oldest surviving concert hall in the world), college chapels and the Jacqueline du Pré building at St Hilda's College.

Wren commissioned William Byrd to create the original sculptured heads that surround the Sheldonian. Thirteen of these mysterious 'emperors' adorn the curved railings and a further four stand guard outside the Museum of the History of Science. The museum was the first home of the Ashmolean collection and now houses an excellent collection of historic scientific objects.

There are many intriguing shops around the Broad Street area. Bargain-hunters may want to explore the Oxfam shop – the first permanent charity shop in the UK. Those with a bit more to spend might want to browse in the exclusive shops along Turl Street. But what is quite clear is that if you are a book-lover and you are in Broad Street, you have come to the right place for here and in the surrounding area is a myriad of bookshops.

Waterstone's stands on the corner at the Cornmarket Street end. Borders bookshop and café is a relative newcomer to nearby Magdalen Street. However, the dominant name in Broad Street is Blackwell's with several separate premises and the main store at nos. 48–51. It is incredible to think that the original shop was so tiny it could only hold three customers at any one time. When it opened in 1879 there were already two successful bookshops opposite and Frederick Macmillan reputedly told Benjamin Blackwell that he had 'chosen the wrong side of the street to be successful'. Blackwell's success and expansion proved him very wrong.

Blackwell's Broad Street façade belies the spaciousness beyond: the underground Norrington Room – with three miles of shelving – has to be seen to be believed.

Tel:	01865 792792
Open:	Mon–Sat 0900–1800
	(except Tue opens 0930),
	Sun 1000–1700

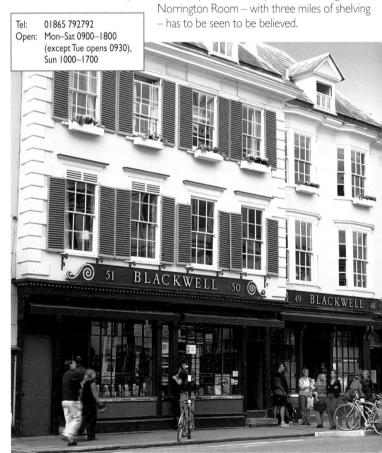

Tel: 01865 728822
Open: Jul–Aug: Daily 0930–1700;
      Sep–Jun: Mon–Sat 1000–
      1630, Sun 1100–1630
      (closed Christmas Day only)

▶ The Oxford Story

Oxford does not only cater for lovers of history, culture or architecture: some attractions are also very popular with younger visitors. The Oxford Story provides an excellent and entertaining introduction to the city's history and the exhibition is a particular favourite with children.

Created by the same group that was responsible for the Jorvik Viking Centre, the tour begins with an audio-visual introduction to student life in Oxford. Then it is time to climb aboard your medieval-desk 'time-car' (pictured on back cover) for a journey back into the city's history. One of Europe's longest 'dark' rides takes you through the sights and sounds of Oxford from medieval times to the present day. The scene above depicts the St Scholastica's Day riot, one of the most notorious encounters between town and gown. On the Feast of St Scholastica in 1355, scholars were drinking in the Swyndlestock Tavern at Carfax (a sign on the current Abbey National building shows where the tavern was). They argued with the landlord and threw wine at his head. There had always been tensions between the town and the university and the townspeople's anger was roused by this latest insult. A bloody fight spilled onto the streets and lasted for three days. More than 60 students were killed. In the end the mayor and citizens had to swear allegiance to the chancellor of the university and do penance for many hundreds of years.

Thomas Cranmer, Archbishop of Canterbury from 1533, was responsible for annulling two of Henry VIII's marriages and for divorcing him from a third. Following Mary's ascension to the throne, Roman Catholicism was reintroduced and between 1555 and 1558 approximately 300 people were executed as heretics. Bishops Latimer and Ridley were burned at the stake in the town ditch in October 1555. Cranmer recanted his Protestant faith but was told that he was still to be put to death. Standing on a platform in St Mary's, he retracted the recantation, swearing that he would first punish the hand that had written against his beliefs. Before he was burned at the stake in Broad Street, Cranmer put his right hand into the flames. The spot is marked by a simple cross in the street-paving and a plaque on the wall of Balliol College. The Martyrs' Memorial (pictured below) in St Giles was designed by George Gilbert Scott and built in 1841. Cranmer is depicted holding his Bible, which bears the date 1541, the first year of its circulation.

Ironically, the college that dominates St Giles is St John's, where the Catholic martyrs St Edmund Campion and Archbishop William Laud were, respectively, a brilliant scholar and college president. Laud was responsible for financing the elaborate Canterbury Quad which leads to the college gardens. He was also responsible for the 'Laudian Code' – a set of rules that, for example, forbade students to gamble, smoke, drink, play football, wear their hair in curls or 'idle and wander about the city or its suburbs, nor in the streets or public market or Carfax'.

St Giles is the main route into Oxford from the north. For two days every September, this route is blocked to traffic to make way for one of the city's great traditions – St Giles' Fair.

St John's College	
Tel:	01865 277300
Open:	Daily 1300–dusk

University Museum of Natural History and Pitt Rivers Museum

The unconventional Gothic façade of the building opposite Keble College conceals a surprise, for it fronts not one excellent museum – but two!

The University Museum of Natural History was begun in 1855 with the aim of showing the history of life on earth. The building had many critics – Tennyson described it as 'perfectly indecent'. The O'Shea brothers who carved all the creatures on the exterior were reputedly fond of including the features of any academics who upset them – it is probably our loss that the brothers were asked to destroy these caricatures!

The museum itself houses dinosaurs, meteorites, a working beehive and thousands of other wonders of the natural world. One of its best-known artefacts is John Savery's painting of a dodo, the Mauritian bird that became extinct in the 17th century and was immortalized by Lewis Carroll in *Alice's Adventures in Wonderland*.

University Museum
Tel: 01865 270949
Open: Daily 1200–1700
Pitt Rivers Museum
Tel: 01865 270949
Open: Mon–Sat 1200–1630, Sun
        1400–1630 (check re
        Christmas/New Year
        closures)

The entrance to the Pitt Rivers Museum is through the University Museum. This museum is an engrossing collection of ethnographic and archaeological artefacts – displayed in cabinets, in drawers, on the walls and hanging from the ceiling. Objects include masks, weaponry, beads, textiles and tools. The museum has a loyal following and children will love the more gruesome exhibits such as the shrunken heads.

The Rivers

Oxford's two rivers, the Isis (Thames) and the Cherwell, played an important role in the city's development and continue to form a large part of its character. Early religious institutions such as Godstow nunnery (ruins of which survive today) and the once-mighty Oseney Abbey were situated near the Isis. The city's name probably derives from its river setting: the place where oxen 'forded' the river. Today the rivers provide a source of pleasure and sport for both students and locals. The two important dates on the university rowing calendar are Torpids (in the spring or 'Hilary' term) and Eights Week (in the summer or 'Trinity' term). The Head of the River pub by Folly Bridge owes its name to its situation near the race finishing line. The boat that wins is 'head of the river'.

A less exerting way to travel is by punt, provided someone else is doing the punting! It was the Victorians who kept the practice alive – by using punts as leisure, rather than simply working, boats. Today, punting has almost died out outside Oxford and Cambridge where it is one of the highlights of the summer. Those who are new to punting usually start from Magdalen Bridge and punt up the Cherwell. At the weir beyond Mesopotamia (a walk between two strands of the river) they must either turn back or push their punt over the metal tracks known as 'the Rollers' to travel further upstream. Locals are more likely to start from the Cherwell Boathouse in Bardwell Road, North Oxford.

And for those who prefer to enjoy the water without actually being in it, there are many delightful walks alongside the rivers or canal.

Ashmolean Museum

Many fascinating artefacts are waiting to be sought out behind the classical façade of the university's Ashmolean Museum.

The world-famous Ashmolean collection began with 'The Ark', a collection of curiosities from around the world collected by John Tradescant and his son, also called John. Elias Ashmole persuaded the Tradescants that he should be the curator of their collection after their deaths and eventually passed the collection to the university, in accordance with the Tradescants' wishes. These pieces from the original 'Ark' are among the most intriguing – representing some of history's most significant figures and periods. They include Cranmer's shackles, Guy Fawkes' lantern and a mantle belonging to Powhattan, the father of Pocahontas.

The most famous piece in the museum consists of a small enamel figure depicted under crystal in a gold frame. Known as the Alfred Jewel, it is a Saxon piece that would have been fixed to a pointer to follow text in a manuscript. It bears the inscription *Aelfred mec heht gewyrcan* or 'Alfred had me made'. The Alfred that is thought to have commissioned it is of course Alfred the Great.

The Ashmolean also has a renowned art collection including Uccello's *Hunt in the Forest*, drawings by Raphael and Michelangelo and a selection of Dutch, Pre-Raphaelite and Impressionist works.

Tel:	01865 278000
Open:	Tue–Sat 1000–1700, Sun 1400–1700, Mon closed; check for late-night opening in summer months

From Worcester to Gloucester

There is a high concentration of colleges in the city centre, but several more are situated just outside. Lady Margaret Hall, the first academic hall for women at Oxford, lies next to the splendid University Parks and has beautiful gardens. St Catherine's College, which enjoys a riverside setting to the northeast, is either an eyesore or an architectural triumph, depending on your point of view. Its Danish architect Arne Jacobsen had the challenge of designing a modern college with traditional features. St Hilda's – the one remaining women-only college – also lies on the banks of the picturesque River Cherwell.

Worcester College lies to the west and is a real delight, with wonderful gardens and its own lake. The college was founded in the 18th century and has much neoclassical architecture. However, a former Benedictine Hall was sited here and a row of medieval cottages has survived. The tunnel at the end of these cottages leads to Worcester's renowned gardens and it is to this that Lewis Carroll was referring when he described how Alice looked along the 'small passage' that led 'into the loveliest garden you ever saw'.

To reach Worcester College you may pass through the pedestrian area known as Gloucester Green (pictured below). This was once the site of a busy cattle market so it is appropriate that it now plays host to the regular open-air market (on Wednesdays) and a smaller fleamarket (on Thursdays). 'Curioxity', a hands-on science exhibition for children, is just around the corner in George Street.

Lady Margaret Hall
Tel: 01865 274300
Open: Daily 0900–1600 (term time, gardens only)

St Catherine's College
Tel: 01865 271700
Open: Grounds open during daylight hours

St Hilda's College
Tel: 01865 276884
Open: Daily 1400–1700

Worcester College
Tel: 01865 278300
Open: Summer: Daily 1400–1700; Winter: Daily 1400–dusk

Curioxity
Tel: 01865 247004
Open: Sat–Sun and local school holidays 1000–1600

Oxford Pubs

If the wealth of sights and culture gets too much, then you could always follow the example of J.R.R. Tolkien, Richard Burton and Inspector Morse – slip into your favourite pub!

Will you be able to negotiate your way to the Turf Tavern? This former malthouse is only reached via either of two winding alleyways – Bath Place or St Helen's Passage (formerly Hell Passage). 'The Turf' has a small, cosy interior but a large and popular beer garden.

The 'Inklings' – a group of writers and drinkers including C.S. Lewis and Tolkien – used to meet regularly in the charming Eagle and Child pub on St Giles. Lewis and Tolkien also enjoyed a drink in the Eastgate Hotel on the High Street.

On the opposite side of the High Street stands the Mitre, which has been a pub since 1310. A secret tunnel used to link the Mitre with buildings across the street, and it is said that both ends were bricked up – trapping a group of monks – during the Dissolution of the Monasteries.

The Bear, on Alfred Street, is one of Oxford's oldest pubs and one of its more eccentric, having a collection of over 5,000 ties. In the past unsuspecting customers were in danger of having any unusual ties snipped off!

Some of Oxford's best-loved pubs are outside the centre – often in a riverside setting. These include the Trout at Godstow, the Perch at Binsey and the Victoria Arms at Old Marston.

Oxford's best-known detective was familiar with a number of Oxford's pubs! Find out which ones on the Inspector Morse guided tour (from the Tourist Information Centre every Saturday at 1.30 p.m.).

Visitors may be interested in a walking tour of the city.
A number of informative and entertaining guided walking
tours depart daily from the Oxford Tourist Information
Centre – contact them for details.
Tel: 01865 726871
Open: Mon–Sat 0930–1700 (all year), Sun 1000–1530
         (Easter to Oct)

CITIES & REGIONS
and
AERIAL GUIDES

Available by mail order
For free colour brochure and full stock list, contact:
Jarrold Publishing,
Healey House, Dene Road, Andover,
Hampshire, SP10 2AA, UK.
Enquiries: 01264 409200
Sales: 01264 409206 • Fax: 01264 334110
e-mail: heritagesales@jarrold.com   website: www.britguides.com

UNICHROME
ISBN 1-871004-93-4

9 781871 004939